THE ORGANIC HANDBOOK 1

How to make your Garden Fertile

Building a healthy soil with compost and manures

Pauline Pears

Henry Doubleday Research Association / Search Press

The Author would like to thank Bob Crowder who introduced her to Sir Albert Howard; to Dick Kitto who inspired her compost making; and to Ned who activates it!

First published in Great Britain 1990
Search Press Ltd.
Wellwood, North Farm Road,
Tunbridge Wells, Kent TN2 3DR.

in association with

The Henry Doubleday Research Association,
National Centre for Organic Gardening,
Ryton-on-Dunsmore,
Coventry CV8 3LG.

Illustrations by Polly Pinder
Photographs by Charlotte de la Bedoyère with the exception of the following, whom the Publishers would like to thank: Animal Aid for the photographs of pigs and battery chickens on page 16; HDRA for the photographs of alfalfa and crimson clover on page 41 and the photograph of bitter lupin on page 42.

The Publishers would also like to thank Mrs. H.A.C.T. Clark for allowing them to photograph her hedgehog, which appears on page 46.

ISBN 0 85532 673 5

Typeset by Scribe Design, 123 Watling Street, Gillingham, Kent
Printed in Spain by Elkar S. Coop. Autonomia, 71-48012-Bilbao-Spain.

Conversion Charts

From centimetres to inches		From grammes to ounces
1 cm	= ½ in	5 g = ¼ oz
2.5 cm	= 1 in	10 g = ½ oz
5 cm	= 2 in	25 g = 1 oz
10 cm	= 4 in	100 g = 4 oz
50 cm	= 20 in	
100 cm (1 m)	= 40 in	
1 sq.m	= 1.2 sq.yds	

Exact conversions from Imperial to Metric measures are not possible, so the Metric measures have been rounded up.

Introduction

The basis of effective organic growing is a well cared for soil – a soil with a good structure, rich in plant foods and teeming with life. The way to build and maintain such a soil, whatever the original soil type, is to feed it with what are called 'bulky organic materials', i.e. bulky materials of animal or vegetable origin, such as compost, manures and leaf mould. These materials cannot be bought off the shelf in a garden centre, or used in neat handfuls straight from the bag, which means that they are not used as much as they might, or should be.

The aim of this book is to encourage more gardeners to get away from the 100 g per sq metre, chemical fertiliser syndrome by pointing out the benefits of using these 'bulky organic materials', and by providing practical advice on how to do so. Gardens vary in size from tiny window boxes to large plots of an acre or more. Even in a small garden there are plenty of items that can be recycled which will help keep your soil fertile. You cannot entirely rely on these, but other things can be brought in from outside to supplement them.

Whatever the size of your garden, this book contains methods which will help you make it organically fertile. Beginning with an explanation on the composting process, the book goes on to describe what can and cannot be composted, detailing both materials of vegetable origin and the usefulness of various types of animal manure. There is a section on how to contain, site and build your compost heap, which is followed by instructions on how to make worm compost and leaf mould, and a section on how to use straw, hay and woodland materials.

Organic materials can either be dug into the soil, or spread as a surface mulch, and both of these methods are discussed in the section on 'Using organic materials in the garden'. Finally there is a section on green manures. These are plants that are grown specifically to benefit soil structure and fertility. If used regularly they can have a remarkable effect on the soil and the plants that grow in it.

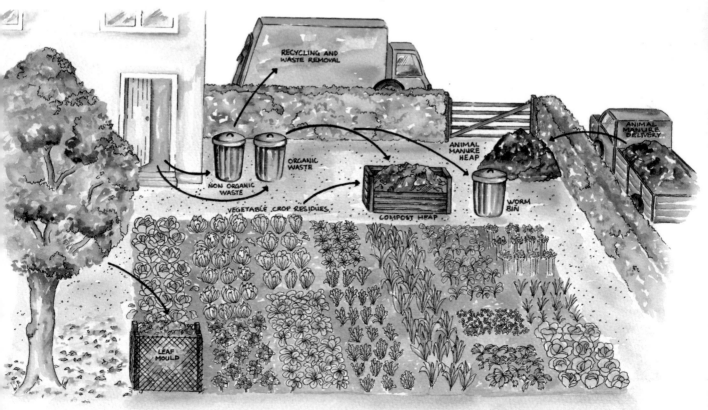

This is a book that should be of interest to all gardeners, whatever the size of their plot. The importance of a good soil does not diminish with the dimensions of the garden.

The organic option

Plant foods

In an organic garden, we talk about feeding the soil, not feeding the plants. Although the soil may look lifeless, it is far from it, but as most soil-living creatures are on a microscopic scale they tend to go unnoticed. It is these tiny creatures that manage the soil for us, which is why it is important to keep them well supplied with their favourite foods – manures, composts and other organic materials. As they feed they release a slow, steady supply of a whole range of plant foods, from the major elements right down to the trace elements, which can be used by growing plants. The result is a sturdy balanced plant which is less attractive to pests and diseases.

Soil structure

The benefit of bulky organic materials is not limited to the plant foods they supply; they are also good for the physical structure of the soil. Their tougher components, which take a long time to decompose, are combined with soil particles by the action of earthworms and other soil-living creatures. In light soils this increases the amount of water and plant foods that the soil can hold on to, so it does not dry out so quickly and becomes more fertile.

Heavy soils tend to be wet and sticky because they are made up of tiny soil particles that stick together in large clumps, with no spaces between for air or drainage. Organic materials help to break the large clumps into smaller 'crumbs', which makes for better drainage, allows more air into the soil and helps to make available the store of plant foods the soil contains. Such a soil will become easier to work and will be an easier environment for plants to grow in.

A good soil structure encourages vigorous, extensive root growth – which results in a sturdy, self-sufficient plant, strong enough to withstand a fair amount of adversity.

Soil health

Organic materials will also help to keep a soil healthy by supporting an active and diverse soil community, where no one particular organism, be it pest or disease, is likely to get out of hand; and because plants are encouraged to grow more strongly, they will be more able to survive an attack.

The whole process is quite miraculous and one that we humans can take no credit for at all. It is just what nature has been doing, with great success, for millions of years.

The chemical option

The chemical option, on the other hand, has only been available for the past fifty years or so, and is very definitely not natural. Artificial fertilisers bypass the soil-living creatures, and disrupt their work. They supply a limited range of plant foods which dissolve quickly in the soil, so they are all available to the plant at once. As a result, plants tend to take up more than they need, especially in the way of nitrates, and the result is lush, watery growth which is just what pests and diseases find most attractive. What the plants don't take up is often washed out of the soil, wasting resources and polluting the environment. And of course, artificial fertilisers contain nothing in the way of organic material, so they do nothing for the structure or health of the soil.

The environmental connection

Plants have been growing naturally for millions of years, without requiring any added fertilisers, and without causing the major pollution that modern agriculture has achieved. This is because everything is recycled and nothing is allowed to go to waste. And this is what organic growers are aiming for – long term sustainability with minimum effect on the environment.

It can never be said that an organic system is completely natural, but it does try to follow nature's example. Materials are recycled wherever possible, taking resources back into the system rather than wasting them.

Composting

Well-matured compost looks and smells just like dark brown crumbly, fibrous soil. It is one of the best materials for feeding the soil and will improve both structure and fertility. All that is needed to make this wonderful substance is a mixture of materials of living origin – materials often regarded as 'leftovers' and 'rubbish', which would normally be wasted and thrown on to yet another rubbish tip, or burnt in polluting bonfires. Compost is recycling at its best.

The first step the would-be composter should take is to stop worrying. Compost-making is a subject often made to sound very complicated, leading to the belief that compost will never work unless everything is 'just right'. In fact this is not the case at all.

The next step is to gain some understanding of the composting process. It is always easier to get something right if you know why you are doing it.

The final step is to get on with it. The first batch of compost may not be the quality that was wished for, and may take longer than desired, but never mind. It will still be useful stuff and the next batch is likely to be better.

In the end, gardeners devise their own system to suit their own particular circumstances.

Understanding the composting process

The composting process is one that is entirely natural. It is carried out by a myriad of creatures, most of them too small to be seen with the naked eye. These useful workers include bacteria, fungi, algae, mites, spring-tails, centipedes, spiders, beetles, slugs and earthworms. It has been estimated that there are around one thousand million microscopic organisms alone in each teaspoonful of compost! Those who are suspicious, or not fond of creepy crawlies should be aware of this when investigating a compost heap while it is working. It is all too easy to imagine that it is full of awful pests, when in fact they are simply legitimate workers!

When suitable materials are heaped up, these 'compost workers' appear as if by magic, and start feeding on the more succulent items. Their numbers increase rapidly in the presence of so much food, and so the rate of decomposition speeds up. As a result of all this activity, heat is produced, which is quite noticeable if the heap is large enough to contain it. In a very hot heap, the oxygen that the composting microbes need may be in short supply after a few days and their work will slow down; turning the heap to introduce more air can start it up again.

Not every heap will heat up, especially those that are made piecemeal. This does not necessarily mean that it will not be composting; it may just be that the rate is too slow to produce much heat, or that the heap is too small to contain it.

Having finished the more tender ingredients of the heap, the bugs move on to the tougher material. The rate of work slows down and the heap cools. At this stage the larger creatures, such as worms, beetles, etc., will move in to help with the work.

By the end of the process, most of the original ingredients of the heap will have been broken down, mixed together and rebuilt into what we know as compost.

What can and cannot be composted

In theory, anything that has once lived can be recycled through the compost heap, though there are certain ingredients that may be best avoided. Anything that has not lived will *not* compost. The chart on pages 18 and 19 lists materials that are suitable for composting, and also those that are not.

When making a compost heap it is important to include a mixture of materials. There must be tough, fibrous (carbon rich) ingredients, to give the end product some body; soft, sappy (nitrogen rich) materials to give the bugs the energy to start the composting process. Too much carbon and the heap will take many years to compost; too many nitrogen rich materials will result in a slimy, smelly heap.

The pictures on the following pages and chart on pages 18 and 19 indicate the properties of each material to help you get this balance right.

Animal manure
A good way of adding bulk to the compost heap.

COMPOST ACTIVATORS

Compost activators are simply anything that will get the composting process started, rather like firelighters help to light a coal fire. These activators are highlighted in the pictures and chart on the following pages.

Natural activators
These are materials that the composting bacteria find easy to digest, providing them with the energy to start on the tougher ingredients. Natural activators tend to be poor in structure and high in nitrogen – such as grass mowings, comfrey leaves, poultry manures, dried blood, urine and nettles. Seaweed is also a good activator as the alginates it contains are an excellent bacterial food.

Activating materials are automatically included in a compost heap if you follow the instructions given in this book – it is not at all essential to add an activator from a packet.

'Packet' activators
These fall into three categories:

a. Soluble nitrogen fertilisers – these are simply chemical fertilisers which provide instant nitrogen.

b. Bacterial products – these supply a range of selected compost bacteria which are said to supplement and improve on those that occur naturally.

c. Herbal materials – a combination of herbs that are said to help the composting process and enhance the end product.

The first type of activator is not acceptable in an organic garden, but the other two may be used. There is not a lot of scientific evidence to show that they have any effect in an amateur compost heap, but many gardeners do seem to find them useful.

Ash, wood

This provides potassium and lime. Do not include coal or other ashes.

Brassica stems

These may have to go through a compost heap several times unless shredded or chopped first, or they can be added to a compost trench, (see page 26).

Blood, dried *Activator*

This usually has to be bought. It contains readily available nitrogen.

Bracken

Green bracken can be cut and added to a compost heap.

Cardboard, newspaper, etc.

Black and white newsprint or cardboard, (torn up), can be composted, though they do not add much goodness. They might be better for recycling. Newspaper can also be used as a mulch. Avoid papers with coloured inks.

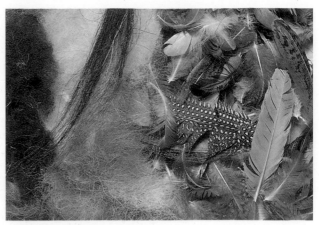

Fabrics, feathers and human or animal hair

Both hair and feathers contain good levels of nitrogen. Pure wool or cotton fabrics, (tattered clothes), can also be used. They should all be moistened well.

Grass cuttings   *Activator*

As thick layers of grass tend to exclude air, mix the cutting up with other materials. Too many mowings will make a heap slimy.

Diseased plant material

There is not a great deal of information available on which diseases do, or do not, survive the composting process. A hot heap, reaching 21°C(70°F) or so should kill many diseases, including onion white rot, as long as the diseased material is put into the middle of the heap. The inclusion of plant material infected with very persistent diseases such as clubroot or tobacco mosaic virus should be avoided.

Diseases that may survive a cool heap will be those that produce resistant spores (such as clubroot and onion whiterot) and those that can survive in dead and decaying plant material, (such as mildews, grey mould and foot rots). The general microbial activity in a compost heap may well reduce or kill such diseases, but there is no hard evidence to support this.

Diseases such as potato blight, which need living plant material to spread from, should pose no problems.

Glass and metal

Anything containing glass or metal will do nothing for your compost heap. It will also make the compost dangerous to handle.

Kitchen animal scraps

Meat, fish and cooked food scraps are best avoided if rats may be a problem.

Hay and straw

Hay contains much more goodness than straw. Old hay composts more quickly than new. Old and/or chopped straw is best. Soak both well if dry. Do not use compost made with straw for tomatoes, peppers, aubergines or cucumbers for a year or so, if there is a risk it may have been sprayed with hormone weedkillers. If large quantities of hay are available, it is best used as a mulch, (see page 37).

Hedge clippings and prunings

Hedge clippings and soft prunings should be mixed with other materials to compost, shredding first if possible. Woody prunings will compost if shredded. Otherwise heap them up in a corner to decay gradually – making a home for wildlife in the process. Conifers and evergreens will tend to make an acid compost.

Kitchen vegetable scraps and crop residues
These all make good compost ingredients.

Leaves, comfrey   **Activator**
These leaves are high in nitrogen and potasssium.

Leaves, autumn
A few autumn leaves may be added to a compost heap. In quantity they are best made into a separate leaf mould heap, see pages 31—33.

Leaves, rhubarb
Although these are poisonous to eat, they are quite safe to compost.

Manure, dog, cat and other pet
Cat and dog manures add valuable nutrients to a compost heap, but they can contain organisms that are harmful to humans and must be used with caution (see page 17). The bedding from rabbits, gerbils, guinea pigs etc., can all go on your compost heap.

Plastics

Never put man-made materials on your compost. This includes every kind of plastic container or wrapping and also synthetic clothes and materials.

Potato haulm

Once you have harvested your potato crop, the haulm can safely be composted. Even blight-infected haulm can be used. Potato tubers, on the other hand, can carry over disease and should not be included.

Nettles   *Activator*

They contain a good selection of plant foods and are high in most minerals.

Seaweed *Activator*

Fresh or dried, the alginates in seaweed encourage bacterial action. It also contains potassium and trace elements.

Soil

There is no need to add soil to a compost heap, except perhaps as a topping. Large amounts of soil can slow down the process, so weed or plant roots with large quantities of soil are best cleaned up before composting.

Weeds, pernicious and perennial

The first reaction to these weeds is not to include them, and this is probably right in the case of the really persistent ones. Three, bindweed, couch grass and ground elder, are pictured above. Others include oxalis and celandine. With less pernicious weeds it seems a shame not to use them as their roots, especially the deep rooted ones, such as docks and dandelions, contain all sorts of useful minerals. Lay them out in the sun to dry for a week or two before composting. Large quantities can be made into a separate heap and left for a year or two, preferably under black polythene to avoid regrowth, until decayed.

Urine *Activator*

This is a good source of nitrogen and potassium. Use diluted 1:3 with water on heaps short of nitrogen. Too much will make the salt level too high for worms to tolerate.

Weeds with seeds

Adding weed seeds to a compost heap usually results in weedy compost, unless it heats to 21°C(70°F) well. If weedy compost is a problem, either avoid adding weed seeds, (although this can be a waste of good material), or use the compost where the weed growth can be easily hoed off.

Mushroom compost

Used mushroom compost is often available quite cheaply and it is relatively clean and pleasant to handle. It can make a good soil conditioner and supplies some plant foods. It does, however, have drawbacks and is not advised for regular use in an organic garden.

Mushroom compost is made from strawy horse manure, with added nitrogen. This is rotted down, sown with mushroom spawn and then covered with a layer of peat and chalk, or ground limestone. These latter ingredients mean that used mushroom com-post has a liming effect on the soil, so it should not be used where the pH is already around 6.5 or higher. On other soils this fact should be taken into account when using it, and it should certainly never be applied to acid-loving plants. The used compost will also contain residues of pesticides used to control pests and diseases in the mushroom crop, unless the grower used organic methods. This really makes it unsuitable for use in an organic garden unless it is stored for six months to a year before use.

Animal manures

Not so long ago, animal manures were regarded as a valuable resource; their role in keeping the soil fertile and productive made them far too useful to waste. It is only over the last fifty years or so that manures have come to be looked upon as unwanted waste products, a problem to dispose of. Modern intensive farming methods allow large numbers of animals to be kept on an area of land far too small to use all the manure produced, and the introduction of artificial fertilisers has meant that most arable farmers no longer want to manure their land.

But just because the majority of farmers no longer value manures does not mean that they have lost their value. The benefits to soil fertility, structure and health, remain the same as they have always been.

In an ideal world, the organic gardener would only use manures from organic farms; but organic farmers use their manures and will rarely have any to spare. The best we can do is to search out sources where animals are kept in relatively humane conditions.

Manures to avoid are those from intensive farms such as battery chicken houses and piggeries. These manures can smell quite awful, and are likely to be contaminated with antibiotics (used to try to keep the animals healthy in their overcrowded conditions), growth promoters and heavy metals such as copper and zinc.

Battery chicken manure
This smells awful and is probably contaminated with antibiotics, heavy metals and growth promoters.

Free-range chicken manure
If you can get manure from free-range chickens, or any other poultry (pigeons, turkeys, geese, ducks, etc.), that are not kept intensively it will be a valuable source of nitrogen, (see page 17).

Intensive farm manure
Avoid manures from intensive farms such as piggeries, cattle farms, etc. They may be contaminated with heavy metals (such as copper), antibiotics and growth promoters.

Cow manure
You may be able to obtain manure from a local dairy and cattle farmer. It is a valuable commodity and worth looking for. Ponies, horses and donkeys, if kept humanely, are another valuable source. Try riding schools.

Good places to try for manure are stables and riding schools, which seem to be increasing in number. These are often close to towns (or sometimes even within the large cities) and are likely to regard the ever-growing piles of manure as an embarrassing problem. If you are prepared to fill your own sacks, this manure may often be obtained free of charge.

Some dairy and cattle farmers may still be prepared to deliver a trailer-load of manure; a local allotment society might be able to suggest one or two. Other possible sources of supply are city farms, pigeon lofts, rabbit farms or fanciers, and even a passing circus.

Manure is such a valuable commodity that it is worth taking some time to search out a supply; it is amazing what you can find once you start looking.

Strawy manures

Horse and cattle are the most commonly available manures and they usually come mixed with strawy bedding material. The analysis of the plant foods these manures contain may make them look rather useless in comparison with a bagged fertiliser, but this is no reason to reject them. They are applied at much higher rates than fertilisers, and their value is not limited to the plant foods they contain. Strawy manures are also particularly good for soil structure.

Goat, donkey and even elephant manures tend to be mixed with straw, and may be available in some areas; they should be treated in the same way as horse and cattle manures, see 'processing and storing' below.

Straw stables manure
Providing it comes from an organic source, strawy manure is good for the structure of the soil.

Processing and storing strawy manures

Fresh manure should be allowed to rot or compost before it is used. This will help to stabilise the nitrogen and potassium it contains, and should also help to reduce any chemical residues. Small quantities of fresh

---

Fresh strawy manures

Fresh strawy manure should not be used directly on the garden for several reasons:

● Fresh manure contains nitrogen in a form that is instantly available to plants, acting in effect like an artificial fertiliser.

● Nitrogen and potassium are easily washed out of fresh manure. This is a waste of plant foods and may also cause pollution.

● Fresh manure contains nitrogen in a form which can burn tender leaves.

● Unless the manure is from organic sources, the straw is likely to contain residues of weedkillers and pesticides.

manure can be processed through a compost heap, larger quantities are usually stacked up on their own. As the stack is built, the manure should be trodden down, or whacked with a spade, to get rid of excess air. It is then covered with a sheet of polythene to prevent rain washing out the goodness; something like half the nitrogen and some valuable potassium can be washed out of an uncovered heap. Inevitably some liquid will drain out even from a covered heap, so it makes sense to site a manure stack where future plants could benefit from it.

After a month or two the heap will have decreased in size, and the manure should be well rotted. If it is not, the problem may be too much straw and not enough manure, which can happen if the manure is from stables which are cleaned out frequently. The answer here is to add more nitrogen, (in the form of poultry manure, grass mowings or urine, for example), or just to use it as a surface mulch. Alternatively the heap may have been too dry, in which case there may be signs of a white fungus, called fire fang, through the manure. The answer here is to take the heap apart, soak it well, and remake it.

Fire fang
This is a fungus which appears in a manure heap which is too dry.

Little is known about how long chemical residues may persist in manures, but it is usually recommended that manure from non-organic sources is rotted for at least six months before use.

If the manure arrives already well rotted, it can be used straight on the garden. If it is not to be used immediately it should be stacked up under cover as described.

Shavings-based manures

Many stables these days keep their horses on woodshavings rather than straw. This makes the manure much easier to handle, but brings with it the potential of those dread words 'nitrogen robbery'. Wood shavings are very high in carbon and contain very little nitrogen; if they are added to the soil without

---

Shavings-based manures

● Be choosy. Always look before you buy. If the manure seems to be comprised mostly of dry shavings, don't get it, or use it as a mulch on pathways. This sort of manure comes from stables that are cleaned out very frequently; there may be another source locally which will contain a higher proportion of urine and 'droppings'.

● Ask the stables' owner if any other gardeners use their horse manure; if so try and have a chat with them.

● Unless it is obviously well rotted – a nice dark colour, with individual shavings not particularly noticeable – do not use it immediately. Stack it up under a plastic cover and leave it to rot for six months to a year.

● To increase the nitrogen content, mix in grass mowings while stacking up a heap to rot, and/or water it all with dilute urine. If you have a compost tumbler, fill this 50:50 (approximately depending on the nitrogen content of the manure) with shavings, manure and grass, turning it daily until it has stopped heating, then empty out the contents and stack them to rot.

● Compost worms in a heap are a sure sign that it is useable.

● When in doubt, use with caution. Try it first of all as a surface mulch on perennial borders where it will not be dug in, adding first a dressing of hoof and horn, or other organic sources of nitrogen, if the soil is poor. It could also be used as a mulch in the vegetable garden on peas and beans (that fix their own nitrogen). Before digging it in over a large area, treat a small test patch and then grow mustard on it, with an untreated patch of mustard for comparison. The growth of the mustard should soon indicate any problems.

sufficient nitrogen, the microbes rob the soil of its available nitrogen so they can get to work on the shavings. Eventually, when the wood has been decomposed, the nitrogen will be made available again, but this can take a year or two. In the meantime the shortage of nitrogen will cause plants to be yellow and stunted.

This should not put people off using a shavings-based manure; it can be a useful source of organic material. The HDRA has had reports from gardeners who have used it for years with wonderful results. The main advice is to use it with caution, following the instructions opposite.

Sheep manure

This is not one of the commonly available manures and, as sheep are rarely kept inside, it usually comes without bedding material. It is best used as a compost activator mixed with water to make a slurry first, or made into a liquid manure.

Sheep and goats are rarely kept intensively. Their manure is high in nutrients.

Pet manures

Rabbits, gerbils, guinea pigs and other domestic pets may not produce vast amounts of manure, but that is no reason to waste it. Whether the bedding be straw, hay or newspaper, it can be added to the compost heap or worm bin with everything else.

The only pet manures to be cautious with are cat and dog. Both these manures can add valuable nutrients to a compost heap, *but* they can also contain organisms that are harmful to humans. Very little research has been done into the fate of these organisms in the compost heap, but it is likely that some of them may survive the process. If dog or cat manure is added to a compost heap, the resulting compost should be handled with care and attention to hygiene. To be on the safe side its use should be restricted to ornamental plants and it should not be used in any situation where young children, who may eat soil, are present.

Poultry manures

Poultry manures contain much higher levels of nitrogen than other manures, and they should not be used directly on the garden. The large amounts of quickly-available nitrogen they contain can lead to lush sappy growth which is much prone to pest and disease attack – not what the organic gardener is looking for! And there is always a risk of damage to tender plants.

Poultry manures make fiery compost heap activators, kept dry in a bin until needed for use. On a larger scale, neat chicken or pigeon manure can be stacked up, in alternate layers, with wet straw, covered over with polythene and then left to rot. The manure provides the nitrogen, the straw the fibre, and the results can be excellent.

In the chicken house, the manure can be dried out and the nitrogen made less readily available by sprinkling the floor with wood ash or finely ground rock phosphate. The mixture can then be used directly on nitrogen-loving crops such as brassicas and potatoes, at a maximum rate of 110 g/sq metre. But don't overdo it! Soil can become *too* rich in nitrogen, at which point nothing much other than nettles will grow.

How it will compost – at a glance

Materials	Structural stability – adds bulk to the final compost	Soft sappy materials – mix with stemmy tough materials	Good balance of nitrogen and carbon	Stemmy tough materials – mix with soft sappy materials	Comments
Blood, dried	Poor	✓	–	–	Add sparingly
Bracken	Medium	–	✓ Young fronds	✓ Older fronds	Cut when green. Do not collect when producing spores.
Brassica stems	Good	–	–	✓	May have to go through compost heap several times unless shredded or chopped first – or add to a compost trench instead. (Do not add roots if club rooted.)
Cardboard (See paper)					
Diseased plant material					A hot heap should kill many diseases. See page 8 for more information.
Fabrics	Poor	–	✓	–	Do not add synthetics
Feathers	Poor	✓	–	–	Can contain over 15% readily available nitrogen. Add sparingly.
Glass					
Grass cuttings	Poor	✓	–	–	Too many make a heap slimy. Excess mowings can be used as a good moisture retaining soil mulch.
Hair, human and animal	Medium	–	✓	–	Contains good levels of nitrogen. Moisten well. Takes a long time to decompose.
Hay	Good	–	✓	–	Contains more goodness than straw. Soak well if dry. For large quantities see pages 9 and 37.
Hedge clippings (see 'prunings, woody')					
Kitchen scraps	Variable	Variable	Variable		Generally a useful addition. Best mixed with other ingredients. Meat and fish scraps may attract vermin.
Leaves, autumn	Good	–	–	✓	A few autumn leaves may be added to a heap. In quantity they are best made into a separate leaf mould heap, see page 31.
Leaves, comfrey	None	✓	–	–	A good source of nitrogen and potassium.
Leaves, rhubarb	Poor/medium	✓	–	–	Although these are poisonous to eat, they are quite safe to compost.
Lime					Not necessary as an ingredient of a compost heap.
Manure, cow and horse with straw bedding	Good	–	✓	✓•	• Properties will depend on how much bedding there is with the manure, see page 15.
Manure, horse with shavings bedding	Good	–	–	✓	Use with caution, see page 16.
Manure, pet					See page 17.
Manure, pig with straw	Good	✓	✓	–	Use only from non intensive farms where growth promoters are not used.
Manure, poultry with bedding	Medium/good	✓	✓	–	Properties will depend on how much manure there is with the bedding

Materials	Structural stability – adds bulk to the final compost	Soft sappy materials – mix with stemmy tough materials	Good balance of nitrogen and carbon	Stemmy tough materials – mix with soft sappy materials	Comments
Manure, poultry without bedding	Poor	√	–	–	Pigeon and chicken manure are very high in nitrogen. Goose and duck manures less so. Use sparingly.
Manure, sheep	Poor	√	–	–	See page 17.
Metal					
Nettles, young	Poor	√	–	–	Contains a good selection of plant foods. High in most minerals.
Nettles, old	Medium	–	√	–	
Paper, cardboard					Torn up black and white newsprint can be composted, though it does not add much goodness. It is better used as a mulch or collected for recycling. Avoid papers with coloured inks.
Plastics					
Potato haulm	Poor/medium	–	√	–	Even blight infected potato haulm can be safely composted if the heap is hot enough. Potato tubers on the other hand can carry over disease and should not be composted.
Prunings, green	Medium	–	√	–	
Prunings, woody	Good	–	–	√	May have to go through several heaps to decay unless shredded first. Useful for making the base of a heap. Avoid rose, gooseberry and other thorny prunings as the thorns take years to decay.
Sawdust	Good	–	–	→	Small amounts may be added to a nitrogen rich heap but it is best not to as they are slow to decay and can cause nitrogen robbery.
Seaweed	Poor	√	√	–	Fresh or dried, the alginates it contains encourage bacterial action. It also contains potassium and trace elements.
Soil					There is no need to add soil to a heap. Large amounts can slow down the process, so weed or plant roots with large quantities of soil are best cleaned up before composting.
Straw	Good	–	–	√	Old and/or chopped straw is best. If dry, soak well before adding. Do not use compost made with straw for tomatoes, peppers, aubergines or cucumbers for a year or so if there is a risk it may have been sprayed with hormone weedkillers as it can distort growth.
Urine, human	No	√	–	–	A good source of nitrogen and potassium. Use diluted 1:3 with water on heaps short of nitrogen. Too much will make salt level too high for worms to tolerate.
Vegetable crop residues	Medium/ good	This will depend on age and type of crop variable			These make good compost ingredients.
Weeds	This will depend on which weeds and their age				These make good compost ingredients. Do not add pernicious perennials, see page 12.
Wood ash	No				Provides potassium and lime. Do not include coal or other ashes.
Wood shavings (see sawdust)					

Containing and siting your compost heap

The compost heap

The process of composting plant and animal remains is not something that the gardener has invented; it happens naturally all the time. What gardeners have done is to refine the whole thing, making it quicker and more productive to suit the greater needs of the garden.

The first refinement is that all the ingredients are gathered together in a heap, rather than leaving them to lie around on the soil surface where they fall.

The simplest compost heap can be made with no more containment than a carpet to cover it. However, most people do tend to make compost in some form of container or bin because it looks neater than a loose heap, and it can result in a better end product. Compost containers can be purchased ready made; it is also quite easy to make one at home.

> **Benefits of making a compost heap**
> ● It allows mixing of different materials, which gives a better and quicker end product.
> ● It keeps the materials moist, which again speeds up the process.
> ● It allows the heat of the process to build up which can kill pests, diseases and weeds; it also speeds up the decomposition.
> ● It looks neater and tidier.

Make your own container

The New Zealand box

This container is one of the best and illustrates well the various aspects that should be taken into account when building or buying a compost box.

The main disadvantages of the New Zealand box are that it can be quite expensive to make or buy unless scrap wood is available. Also it is difficult to move it around the garden, although it can be dismantled if you are moving to another house. The drawings on pages 22 and 23 illustrate how you can construct your own New Zealand box.

Other home-made compost containers

Other containers can be made more simply and cheaply than the New Zealand Box; some suggestions are made on this page. They all try to follow the basic principles illustrated by the New Zealand Box.

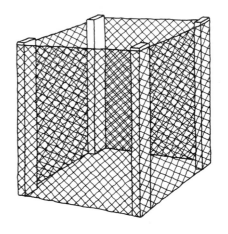

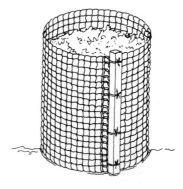

The wire mesh bin: a wire netting container, lined with cardboard or carpet. Cheap and easy to make. This can be square or circular.

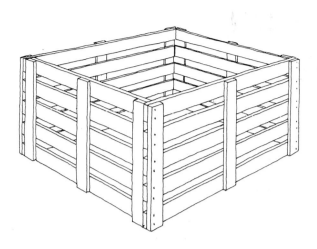

The pallet box: four sides held together with wire. Line with cardboard or carpet. Easy to move.

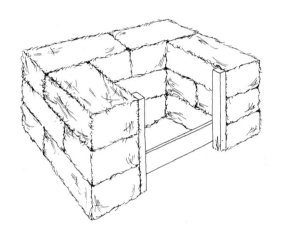

The straw bale heap: if straw bales are available they make an excellent insulated, though short lived, container. It should last a couple of years or so, at which point the straw can be added to the next compost heap!

Commercially available containers

There are some excellent compost containers on the market that are ideal for making really good compost. There are also some inefficient containers. These are usually made by companies that are involved in businesses other than gardening. They feel that their materials can be made into a 'compost box', and give no thought as to whether their containers are actually any good for making compost!

The drawback with many commercial containers is that there are wide gaps in the sides which allow the compost to dry out. This can be overcome with a lining of carpet or cardboard.

Compost tumblers

A compost tumbler is a barrel-shaped container that has some form of framework so that it can be rotated by hand. The container is filled with the same sort of ingredients as the usual heap, left for a few days to allow the composting to start, and then turned several times each day. The turning action of the tumbler ensures that the composting bacteria are never short of oxygen, so they keep working at full speed. The constant mixing ensures that all the ingredients are well composted and that there are no dry edges. This can be very useful when weed seeds or diseased material are being composted. A tumbler has the added benefit of being rat-proof, so materials such as meat scraps can be used.

Compost tumblers tend to heat up very well, and after three weeks or so will produce an immature compost in which the original ingredients will be unrecognisable. At this stage it can be used directly on the garden, or stacked up under cover to mature to a finer product, leaving the tumbler free to be filled again. A tumbler can be usefully used in conjunction with a worm composting bin, (*see page 29*).

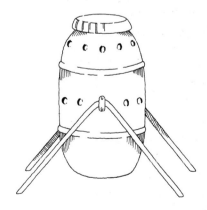

The biggest disadvantage of this method of composting is that it can be hard work. It does take a strong arm, (and back), to turn a tumbler.

How to make a New Zealand box

The instructions on this page show how to construct a two bay New Zealand compost box. The two bays allow you to start a new heap while the previous one is maturing, but you could also use the instructions to construct a single box for one heap.

Complete list of materials

Timber

  9 lengths 10 cm × 1 cm × 1.82 metres
  8 lengths   5 cm × 5 cm × 91.5 cm
27 lengths 10 cm × 1 cm × 97 cm
  6 lengths   5 cm × 5 cm × 1.22 metres
18 lengths 10 cm × 1 cm × 91.5 cm

Other materials

216 2.5 cm nails, 6 7.5 cm nails, 6 13 cm coach bolts (M8) with nuts and 2 washers, 2 old carpets 91.5 cm square, 1 corrugated iron or wooden lid 91.5 cm × 2.74 metres.

1. Back panel

Materials

Timber
9 lengths 10 cm × 1 cm × 1.82 metres (back boards)
3 lengths 5 cm × 5 cm × 91.5 cm (uprights)
Nails
54 × 2.5 cm

Nail back boards to uprights as shown. The central upright is offset 0.5 cm from the centre.

2. Left side panel

Materials

Timber
9 lengths 10 cm × 1 cm × 97 cm (side boards)
2 lengths 5 cm × 5 cm × 1.22 metres (legs)
1 length 5 cm × 5 cm × 91.5 cm (slide)
Nails
54 × 2.5 cm

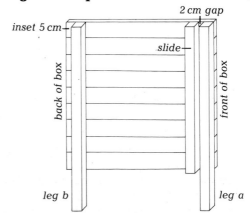

Nail side boards to the 2 legs as shown. Leg a is flush with the ends of the boards. Leg b is inset 5 cm. Nail the slide to the side boards 2 cm in from leg a.

3. Centre panel

Materials

Timber
9 lengths 10 cm × 1 cm × 97 cm (centre boards)
2 lengths 5 cm × 5 cm × 1.22 metres (legs)
3 lengths 5 cm × 5 cm × 91.5 cm (slides)
Nails
54 × 2.5 cm, 6 × 7.5 cm

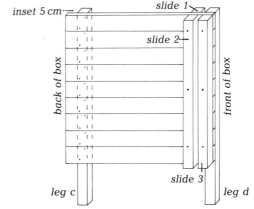

Nail both legs and slide 1 to the centre boards. Set leg c 5 cm in as shown and leg d lies flush with the end of the boards. Slide 1 is set 2 cm away from leg d on the adjacent side of the boards. Fix slide 3 flush to the ends of the boards, using 3 7.5 cm nails which penetrate slide, boards and go into leg d. Fix slide 2 opposite slide 1 in the same way.

4. Right side panel   Materials: as left side panel

Construct in the same way as left side panel, reversing the legs and slide to make a mirror image.

Front (removeable)

Materials

Timber

18 lengths 10 cm × 1 cm × 91.5 cm (boards)
Slot boards into front of boxes

Assembly

Materials

6 × 13 cm coach bolts (M8) with nuts and two washers
Prepare the site by digging 6 holes 46 cm deep to take the legs.
Position panels 2, 3, 4 but do not fill in the holes. Position panel
1; drill holes through panel 1 uprights and back legs of 2, 3 and
4 approximately 3 cm from the top. Insert bolts and tighten.
Drill another set of identical holes approx. 10 cm from the
bottom. Tighten. Slip in the removeable boards at the front.
Now is the time to adjust the position of the legs in the holes so
that the boards fit smoothly in their grooves. When you are
happy with the final position, fill in the holes with rubble
tamping down firmly and top with soil.

N.B. If the bolts are well greased before use they should be
easy to undo at a later date if the box needs to be moved.

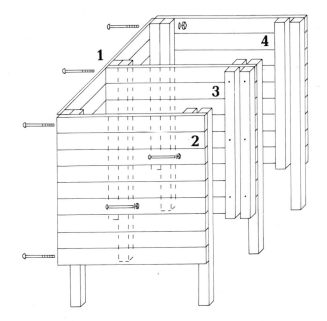

Finished box

wooden construction – sturdy and insulating

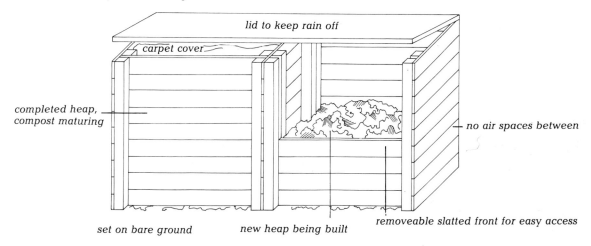

lid to keep rain off

carpet cover

completed heap,
compost maturing

no air spaces between

set on bare ground   new heap being built   removeable slatted front for easy access

Siting the container

A compost container should always sit on
bare soil to allow adequate drainage. The
best place for it is a warm sunny spot,
sheltered from the wind … but this is
probably just where the garden seat lives, so
the compost may have to be relegated to
somewhere not quite so suitable. Remember
to leave sufficient space around the bin to
allow easy access with a barrow. Also, allow
enough space for stacking ingredients before
a heap is built, and an area for emptying the
contents, if the heap is to be turned.

A fair amount of goodness will drain out of
the bottom of a compost heap however good
the mixture of materials; an alternative to
having a static box is to have one that can be
moved round the garden, so that the goodness is not wasted. Greedy feeding plants
such as courgettes and pumpkins will thrive if
grown where a compost bin has been situ-
ated.

Making garden compost

So far we have looked at ingredients and containers for a compost heap. The next step is just to go ahead and start, bearing in mind always the importance of using a mixture of materials, as outlined in the section 'What can and cannot be composted' on page 6. Two further ingredients, which have had scant attention so far, but which are essential to the creatures involved in the composting process, are air and water. Both are incorporated in the heap as it is made.

Air

A heap of mixed ingredients should automatically contain sufficient air. The stemmier items keep air spaces open, while the soft sappy ones, which tend to slump together, make sure that the heap is not so airy that it dries out. Firm down a freshly built heap, but do not squash all the air out of it.

Water

It is difficult to advise on just how much water, if any, needs to be added to a heap. As usual 'it depends', and it is something you will learn by experience. Not enough and the heap will not compost; too much and it will go slimy and become airless! The higher the proportion of sappy material in the heap, the less the need to add water. Weed and crop residues collected shortly after a rain storm are ideal, but if there has been a dry spell these should be watered as they are added to the compost. Very dry ingredients, such as straw or hay, are best soaked well before being added.

Building a compost heap

The simplest method

The simplest way of making compost is to pile up kitchen and garden rubbish as it becomes available, either in a container or in a heap covered with carpet to keep the moisture in. At some point a decision has to be made to stop adding to the heap. It is then turned and mixed up well with a fork. Matted material can be teased out to allow air in; water and/or activating ingredients can be added if required. If the heap is very wet and soggy at this stage, try and add some tougher ingredients to improve the structure.

This sort of heap may not heat up. It may take a while to compost and the end product might not be the best of quality, but as long as it has had a reasonable mixture of ingredients, it should be useable.

Building a better heap

The next step up is to build a heap, or fill a compost bin, in as few stages as possible. The more that can be added to a heap at once, the more likely you are to achieve a good mixture of ingredients. This in turn improves the chances of some heating up, and will help speed the process.

With a bit of planning it should be possible to collect together a good supply of weeds, (a slightly delayed weeding means more for the compost), lawn mowings, kitchen waste and any other materials that are available over a few days. Planning to make a heap in this way tends to encourage forays to find other ingredients, such as a sack of animal manure, waste from the greengrocers or even some seaweed. Green materials can be stored stacked and covered, (so they don't dry out), or in plastic sacks with the air squeezed out. It is said that kitchen waste can be collected over a period or weeks in plastic sacks too, but the result is often rather smelly and unpleasant. Mixing the kitchen waste with dry material such as old potting compost or shredded newspaper can help.

Even though this heap is being built in several stages, its construction should follow the basic instructions given on this page, for the ideal heap.

Of course a compost heap sinks as it decomposes, so it is likely to take an extremely long time to fill a container completely. The answer is just to decide to stop adding to it after a while. Once the last batch of material has been added, the heap can just be left to get on with it; or it can be turned out, remixed and replaced as described for the 'simplest method', adding water and/or an activator material if necessary.

The ideal heap

The ideal way to make compost is to build a complete heap all at one go. Collect all the available ingredients together so that you have a good mixed heap, then start to build up the heap as shown. The individual ingredients can be added in layers; this helps to give an idea of the relative proportions being added. Layering is not essential though; in fact it is more efficient to have everything well mixed together.

The ideal heap

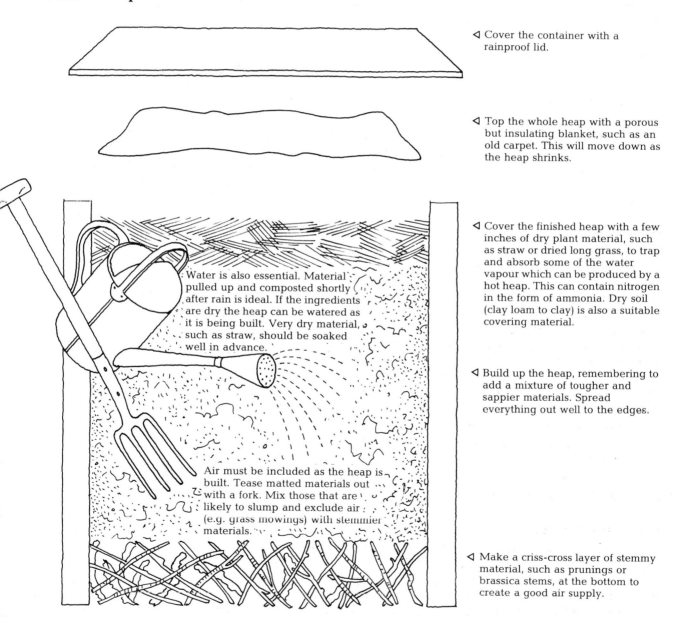

◁ Cover the container with a rainproof lid.

◁ Top the whole heap with a porous but insulating blanket, such as an old carpet. This will move down as the heap shrinks.

◁ Cover the finished heap with a few inches of dry plant material, such as straw or dried long grass, to trap and absorb some of the water vapour which can be produced by a hot heap. This can contain nitrogen in the form of ammonia. Dry soil (clay loam to clay) is also a suitable covering material.

◁ Build up the heap, remembering to add a mixture of tougher and sappier materials. Spread everything out well to the edges.

◁ Make a criss-cross layer of stemmy material, such as prunings or brassica stems, at the bottom to create a good air supply.

Water is also essential. Material pulled up and composted shortly after rain is ideal. If the ingredients are dry the heap can be watered as it is being built. Very dry material, such as straw, should be soaked well in advance.

Air must be included as the heap is built. Tease matted materials out with a fork. Mix those that are likely to slump and exclude air (e.g. grass mowings) with stemmier materials.

Speeding up the process

Chopping and shredding

The smaller the pieces in the compost heap, the easier it is for the compost workers to act on them, and so the quicker the end product. This is especially true of tough materials such as old cabbage stems or soft prunings which need several 'goes' through a compost heap before fully decomposing. Chopping up less tough material can be helpful and makes for a finer end product.

The usual way to chop compost materials is to lay them out on the ground, (not a hard surface), and chop with a sharp spade. This is quite hard work and time consuming; or run a garden roller over tougher items laid out on a concrete path. This will not chop them, but it will start to break them up.

Compost shredders The easiest way to chop up compost material is to use a shredder. There are several makes available to the gardener, both petrol and electrically driven. A shredder can even reduce such materials as old raspberry canes and woody prunings, (not normally composted), to a pile of small wood chips in no time at all. These are perfect for composting.

The main disadvantage of a shredder is the price. They can be quite expensive so it may be tempting to buy a model that is rather less powerful than is needed. However, using a model which is not powerful enough for the job can be an exasperating business. The ideal is something slightly more powerful than might seem to be needed; it is sensible to think carefully about a shredder's uses before buying it.

Turning the heap

When a compost heap heats up, it will reach a maximum temperature, (which can be as high as 21°C[70°F]), after a few days and then it will begin to cool down. If the heap is then taken apart and rebuilt — preferably with the material from the sides now in the middle — it will heat up again. The cooling down is caused because the oxygen supply to the composting bacteria is getting low. The second heating happens when the supply is replenished. This process can be repeated two or three times and will reduce the composting period considerably. The beneficial effect of turning a heap can be seen most clearly when a tumbler is used, (see page 21).

If a heap is not turned it will still compost but the process will take longer.

When will it be ready?

Compost can be used as soon as it has turned a dark colour and the original ingredients are no longer recogniseable. It may still be rather stringy and lumpy and if a finer product is required it will have to be left longer.

Compost can be ready to use in as little as a couple of months, or it may take a year or more. The time taken will depend on a whole range of factors including air temperatures, the mixture of ingredients, how finely it was chopped, and how long the heap took to build.

The compost trench

It is not easy to make compost successfully in the winter. The supply of ingredients tends to be limited to kitchen scraps and old cabbage plants; add these to a winter compost heap and they just sit there not doing very much.

A compost trench is a simple alternative to the compost heap over winter. In the autumn dig a trench 30 cm × 30 cm where beans or peas will be grown next season. Empty kitchen scraps into the trench. Lightly dust with lime; cover with a good layer of soil.

Once the trench is full, replace any remaining soil, and leave it to settle for a month or two before sowing or planting. The decomposed waste makes an excellent source of plant foods and water for peas and climbing beans. Individual compost 'holes' can be made in the same way and later planted with courgettes and marrows.

A compost trench is also a good way of dealing with the stems of old winter brassicas, especially those that are infested with whitefly or mealy aphids. Chop the stems with a spade and put them into the trench and fill with kitchen waste as before. It is best to grow runner beans on a trench filled with brassica stems. These are strong nitrogen fixers, so there is no risk of nitrogen robbery.

Making worm compost

Every gardener could be running a small herd of animals in the back garden to supply manure to keep the soil fertile. We're not talking here about keeping sheep or cows — after all most gardens wouldn't even support a couple of chickens. What we're talking about is keeping worms!

A herd (or is it a flock?) of worms can be kept in an ordinary plastic dustbin, and fed on kitchen scraps. This is something that even a patio or balcony-sized garden can cope with. The worm manure produced, more usually called worm compost, is a valuable, high quality product particularly useful for container growing.

A worm composting system is contained and does not generate any heat, so very little of the goodness of the ingredients is wasted. In addition, the action of the worm's gut on the material as it passes through gives it an excellent stable structure. Worm compost can be used in the same way as any other compost, (*see page 34 onwards*).

Soil living earthworms

Brandling or compost worms, distinguished from the above by their yellow and reddish brown banding.

What are composting worms?

The worms that are kept for making compost are known as brandling or compost worms. Their Latin name is *Eisenia foetida*. They can be found in most gardens, living in decaying organic material such as piles of leaves, animal manures and mature compost heaps.

Brandling worm 'eggs'.   *Actual size —*

Obtaining the worms

Brandling worms can be obtained from various sources:

● Another working worm bin. The worms multiply quickly, so an established worm bin usually has some to spare.

● A compost heap, or an old heap of manure.

● Fishing tackle shops where they are sold as fishing bait.

Setting up a worm compost system

The container

A plastic dustbin is the easiest container to use. It is cheap to buy, meets all the needs of the worms, keeps the whole thing neat and tidy and is easily moved if necessary. Plastic crates, insulated boxes, fruit boxes or bottomless compost bins are also suitable, as long as they fulfil the requirements listed here.

Requirements for a worm compost container

● Drainage: a worm composting system should not produce a great deal of liquid, but adequate drainage is important. If the container gets too wet, air will be in short supply and the worms could drown.

● Moisture: the container must also retain moisture; worms breathe through their skins, so they do need to be kept moist at all times.

● Cover: this is to keep moisture in and rain out, not to keep the worms in. If conditions are right for them, they will stay where they are.

● A relatively large surface area: worms like to work near the surface, so the larger the surface area the better. Tall thin containers, such as swing bins, are not recommended.

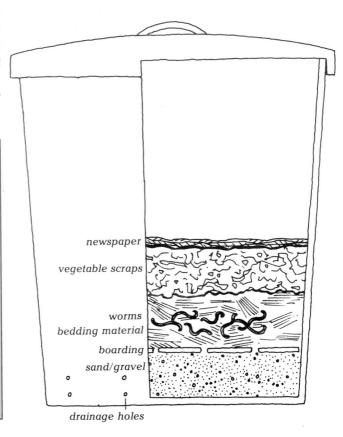

newspaper
vegetable scraps
worms
bedding material
boarding
sand/gravel
drainage holes

Bedding

Until they start making their own compost, the worms need somewhere to live and lay their eggs. They will not do this in uncomposted material, so some form of 'bedding' material must be added at the start. Suitable materials include mature compost or manure or leaf mould or peat mixed half and half with shredded newspaper or cardboard. The bedding material should be damp, but not soggy so that when squeezed in the hand, moisture just drips from it.

Starting your own worm bin

Ideally start a bin with a minimum of fifty to a hundred worms. The more there are the quicker the composting process will get going. It is, of course, possible to start with fewer worms as they breed quite quickly, but in this case it will obviously take longer for the system to really get going.

What do worms eat?

Brandling worms feed on decaying plant material. They can, in theory, be fed with anything that can be put on the compost heap. An ideal source of food for a worm farm is kitchen scraps; worms like to be fed little and often, which is how kitchen scraps are usually available. They will also work their way through tender garden 'rubbish' such as weeds. To increase the output from the bin, rotted manure, or immature compost from a compost tumbler can also be added, but some things are best avoided, as shown in the red box.

Adding the food to the bin

There are various ways in which food is added to a worm bin, all of which seem quite successful.

The food can be put in one corner of the bin and the whole thing covered with wet newspaper. Once worms can be seen colonising this food, another batch can be added in another area. The quantity supplied at one time will depend on the size of the worm box; a 3–4 litre (5¼–7 pints) plastic tubful seems to be a reasonable amount to add to a worm dustbin at one time.

A layer of food, about 10 cm, thick can be placed over the whole area of the box, and covered with a thin sprinkling of bedding material, or a wet newspaper. When this is well colonised with worms, add another layer of food. As a beginner, it is advisable to add food to only one half of the bin at a time, so the worms have somewhere to move to if they do not like the food.

The food can be buried in one part of the bin, just below the surface; when feeding again bury it in another part of the box. The only problem with this method is that it may be difficult to see when a particular batch of food has been colonised by the worms; this is something only experience can teach you.

It is not essential to chop up food before giving it to the worms, but smaller pieces will decompose more quickly. The quantity of fresh material that worms can get through will vary through the year as the temperature and the number of worms alters. When feeding, it is always best to err on the side of caution. If too much food is added at once, it may heat up and drive the worms away. If food is added too often it may begin to putrify before the worms can deal with it. It is usually obvious when this happens; the bin will begin to smell, which a well run bin does not.

If a garden produces too much material for a worm bin to cope with on its own, a second bin can be set up, or the material can be partially composted before it is added to the bin. Material that has been through a compost tumbler is ideal.

The beauty of a worm bin is that there is no need to find a 'sitter' at holiday times. The worms will not die immediately feeding stops. Once all the available food has been used up numbers will begin to decline, but there will be plenty of eggs (small lemon-shaped cocoons) left behind, which will hatch when feeding starts again.

Siting the worm bin

If the worms are to be fed mainly on kitchen scraps, it is useful to have the bin handy. It can be kept in the kitchen, though most people might prefer to keep it outside the house. A sheltered spot, that gets some sun is to be preferred. A bin that is in full sun all day may get too hot, especially in summer. The worms work rate slows down as the temperature reaches the upper 20°C (68°F).

Worms need warmth

Worms also slow down as the temperature drops below 10°C (48°F); they will survive lower temperatures, but will die if they freeze. Because they are so good at dealing with vegetable waste, which can be a problem to dispose of in the winter, it is worth taking some trouble to keep the bin active in the cooler weather. If starting a new bin, do this midsummer at the latest, so there is a good population of worms and bulk of compost in the bin over winter. This will stay active longer than a nearly empty bin.

Extracting the compost

In a working worm bin there will be finished compost, uneaten 'food', and worms. The easiest way to extract the compost is to stop feeding the worms and leave the bin undisturbed for six weeks or so, until most of the food has been used up. Some worms will die off and the rest can be extracted using the method described. Before feeding is stopped, a good scoop of worms, food and compost should be taken out to start a new bin.

If the worm food has always been left on the surface, and the whole mixture has not been stirred up, the majority of uneaten food and worms will be in the top few inches. This worm rich layer can be shovelled out and set aside while the finished compost is taken out, and then replaced to continue the process.

... and the worms

There is no harm in leaving worms in the compost if it is to be used on the garden, though this is rather a waste of useful worms as they do not survive in the soil. If the compost is to be used in pots, it is advisable to extract as many as possible first.

The simplest, most laborious way, is just to pick them out by hand. An easier alternative is to spread the compost out in a layer approximately 10 cm thick, on concrete or a plastic sheet. This is best done on a sunny day. Place a thick layer of wet newspaper in the middle of the spread compost, and leave it. The worms will tend to migrate from the drying compost into the damp shelter under the newspaper.

Making leaf mould

There is nothing more satisfying on an autumn day than raking up the fallen leaves and setting light to them. The smell of burning leaves is quintessential autumn.

But, despite the satisfaction it may afford, burning autumn leaves is the last thing that the organic gardener and the concerned environmentalist should do. The smoke is harmful to health (even more so than cigarette smoke), it pollutes the atmosphere and makes conditions unpleasant for people living in the vicinity. Also, health reasons apart, burning leaves is a waste of money. Why burn them when they can be used on the garden as an excellent free soil conditioner?

In theory, newly fallen autumn leaves can be applied directly to the soil as a surface mulch. This is after all what nature does every year, leaving the task of taking them down into the soil to the worms. The only problem with using leaves in this way is that they are unlikely to stay put. The first of the winter winds will soon send them scattering all over the garden again!

The answer is to make what is know as leaf mould, which is really just rotted leaves. The process is simplicity itself: moist leaves are stacked up and ignored for a year or two. The decay organisms are very different from those involved in a compost heap. In this case they are fungi that are able to slowly work their way through the leaves, despite the very low levels of nitrogen present.

Making a leaf mould heap

It is usual to pile up the leaves in some form of container, but this is only to stop them blowing away. A simple wire mesh cage, for example, is ideal. This should be a minimum of 1 m × 1 m in size, to prevent the heap from drying out, unless it is lined in some way. In a small garden black plastic dustbin bags can be used very effectively.

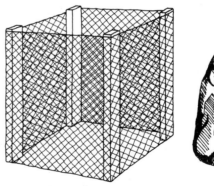 

The ideal time to collect up leaves for a leaf mould heap is after a heavy fall of rain, so that they are well soaked. If this is not possible, they should be watered as they are added to the container. Stuff the bin or bag as full of leaves as possible, to make best use of the space, and that's it!

After a year the leaves will be partially rotted and the heap will have sunk considerably. This young leaf mould can now be used as a mulch for the garden without any danger of it blowing away, or it can be dug into the soil. If a finer product is required, for use in

place of peat in a potting compost for example, the leaves can be left to rot for another year.

The wire mesh enclosure can be removed at this stage, and re-erected elsewhere for another year's leaves, as the heap will now be self-supporting.

Leaves from any deciduous tree (i.e. one that loses its leaves in the autumn) can be used to make leaf mould. Some species may take longer to rot than others, but there is no need to exclude any. Leaves from conifers and other evergreens are best excluded in any quantity unless the leaf mould is to be used on acid-loving plants such as azaleas, heathers, magnolias and blueberries.

Making a quicker leaf mould

The process of making leaf mould can be speeded up by shredding the leaves before heaping them up. A garden 'compost' shredder can be used, or the leaves may just be spread out over a lawn and chopped up with a lawn mower. Any grass that happens to be mixed in with the chopped leaves will also help to speed up the process slightly. If the grass box is left on the lawn mower when mowing, the leaves and grass will be picked up together.

Grass mowings can also be added to a leaf mould heap as it is being built, with mowings making up to 25% of the total. If none are available at the time, a heap can be rebuilt in the spring to include them.

Sources of leaves

The average garden does not yield a great harvest of leaves so, as leaf mould is such a useful product, it is worth taking some trouble to search out other sources of supply. With permission it is sometimes possible to collect leaves from local parks or cemeteries. Some parks departments will even deliver a lorry load to an allotment or other suitable site, for they only have to pay to dump them elsewhere.

You can also collect leaves from quiet streets. The amount of lead that they contain

from petrol fumes is not likely to be significant if they are swept up soon after they have fallen.

It is not advisable to obtain leaves collected up by road sweepers, as they will also contain grit and other roadside debris, with higher levels of pollutants such as lead and cadmium.

The value of leaf mould

Leaf mould is one of the most long-lasting of organic materials. Although it does contain some plant foods, it adds little directly to the soil's fertility because it is so slow to break down. Its main effect is to improve the physical structure of the soil, which in turn results in soils becoming more fertile.

Leaf mould can be used on any soil in almost any part of the garden. It can be either dug in, or applied as a moisture-retaining surface mulch. Fine leaf mould, sprinkled along rows after sowing seeds, can make a considerable different to the emergence of delicate seedlings such as carrots. Spread leaf mould over the grass to improve the soil under a lawn.

Leaf mould is environmentally friendly

Peat and shredded bark are two materials that can be purchased to use as soil conditioners, but neither are as acceptable as leaf mould in an organic garden.

● Peat is not an easily renewable resource; it takes thousands of years to form, and its extraction from the bogs of various parts of the world is destroying tracts of wild countryside.

● Shredded bark is more environmentally friendly, and is certainly preferable to peat. Unfortunately the increased interest in bark products, especially for weed control mulches, has meant that prices have risen rapidly, and it may soon become uneconomic for most gardeners.

Leaves are, of course, free. They will fall whether gardeners use them or not – and the supply is renewed annually. What more could one ask for?

Using compost, manure and leaf mould in the garden

How to apply them

Organic materials can either be dug into the soil, or spread as a surface mulch, which will slowly be taken down into the soil by worms and other soil-living creatures. Both methods have their advantages and disadvantages; the final choice will depend on what is being applied and in what circumstances.

Digging in

When digging in composts and manures, they should be mixed with the top 20 cm of soil only, which is where most of the biological activity goes on; they should never be buried in the depths beyond the reach of most microbes.

> **To dig or not to dig?**
> ● Digging mixes materials in with the soil, giving a quicker overall improvement.
> ● Digging allows compost full of weed seeds to be buried so that the seeds cannot germinate.
> ● Regular digging increases the speed at which the organic material decomposes. This can be counterproductive, especially on light soils, where this is fast enough already.
>
> ● Digging must wait until the soil conditions are suitable.
> ● Digging can be hard work!
> ● Digging in is not suitable for materials that could cause nitrogen robbery.

Mulching

The alternative to digging is to spread the materials in a layer over the soil surface. This is known as mulching. Because a mulch can have an insulating effect on the soil, it should be applied to a soil that is warm and thoroughly wet. Mulch a cold dry soil and it will tend to stay that way.

> **To mulch or not to mulch?**
> ● A mulch keeps the soil moist.
> ● A mulch protects the soil surface structure from damage by rain and prevents it drying out into a hard crust or cap, making seedling emergence easier.
> ● A mulch keeps the soil moist near the surface; this makes it much more attractive for the feeding roots of plants which tend to work in the top few inches of soil.
> ● Mulching is the only way to apply soil-building and feeding materials to perennials such as fruit and shrubs after planting.
> ● Mulching is a suitable method of applying materials that might otherwise cause nitrogen robbery.
> ● Mulches can help to control weeds.
>
> ● As a mulch acts as an insulator it should not be applied when the soil is cold and/or dry. Mulch a cold and/or dry soil and it will tend to stay that way.
> ● Material applied as a mulch will take longer to mix through the bulk of the soil, so its effects will be slower.
> ● Compost full of weed seeds can be a nuisance where other seeds are to be sown.

Timing

To make best use of the plant foods that they contain, and to reduce the risk of any goodness being washed out and wasted, composts and manures are best applied to the soil where plants are, or are about to be growing. On light and medium soils it is usually possible to achieve this. On cold, heavy soils where spring cultivations can be difficult, it may be necessary to apply these materials to some areas in the autumn, when conditions are more favourable.

Where plants are in the ground for some time, such as winter brassicas, an initial application of compost could be dug in before planting, with a top up dressing applied as a mulch after a few months.

Materials such as leaf mould, hay and straw can be applied whenever the soil conditions allow.

How much?

It is easy to overfeed a soil with chemical fertilisers, the result being a reduction in fertility as an excess of one plant food reduces the availability of another. Because the plant foods in *well-rotted* manures and compost come in a balanced mixture and are not in an instantly available form, this 'locking up' of plant foods is unlikely, but it is still possible to overdo the application. If too much manure or compost is applied, the result could be unwanted plant growth (leaf in place of flower or fruit) or unused plant foods being washed out of the soil. In a greenhouse, where there is no rain to wash the soil through, a build up of nutrients can inhibit growth.

How much is too much will depend on the fertility of the soil the plants are growing in and also on the quality of the manure or compost. As a rough (very rough) guide, a barrow-load of compost to 3–4 sq metres of an average soil should be ample for one season, or one 'greedy' vegetable crop.

Materials such as leaf mould, which do not supply much in the way of plant foods, can be used in larger quantities.

What to use where

The problem that most gardeners have is a shortage of compost, manure etc., so the slender resources have to be allocated to those plants that will benefit from them the most.

The following recommendations are for soils that are already in good heart, and do not suffer from any major deficiencies (which must be corrected in other ways). They aim to help the gardener make decisions about what to use where. But the final say-so must be with the person on the spot who knows the soil, and can see what is doing well and what is not.

Well-rotted manure and compost can be used interchangeably in most cases. It is usually the final quality of the product, (e.g. fine or lumpy, weedy or weed-free), which governs what is used where.

Leaf mould, hay and straw may be used on both annual and perennial plants. Woodchip and bark mulches should only be used on perennials, as they could cause nitrogen robbery if they were incorporated into the soil at the end of the season.

Herbs
Many shrubby herbs, thymes for example, thrive in poor dry soil and should not need manure or compost, except on heavy soils where they may benefit from lightening the soil with leaf mould. Succulent herbs, especially chives, parsley and mint do need a good supply of food and water, so may appreciate additions of manure or compost.

Vegetables
A system of crop rotation should be used in the vegetable garden, so that vegetables of the same family are kept together, and move on one bed each year. This means that while the same crops are manured each year, a different area of soil benefits each time, and over a period of years, the whole plot is treated.

The lion's share of any manure or compost should go to the beds growing the following crops: potatoes, tomatoes, brassicas (cabbage family) and other leafy crops, leeks, pumpkins and courgettes. These benefit from both the food and increased water-holding capacity that these organic materials supply. Onions will also appreciate a dressing of compost if it is available.

Some crops benefit particularly from the moisture retaining effects of an organic mulch. This can be manure or compost, or leaf mould if the soil is already rich enough to feed the plants. These crops include Chinese cabbage, celery, celeriac and Florence fennel.

Several crops will grow happily on soil that has been well manured or composted for a *previous* crop. These include carrots, parsnips, beetroot and other root crops. If any compost or manure is used on land that is to grow root crops, it should be a fine, well-rotted material.

On a reasonable soil, peas and beans should not need to be fed, but they do appreciate a lot of moisture once the pods start to form. A thick mulch of leaf mould, hay or straw can be very beneficial.

Herbaceous perennials

A dressing of compost or well-rotted manure every three years should be sufficient. The best time to apply it is when plants are lifted and split up for replanting. A woodland or bark mulch could be used in the intervening years.

Shrubs

A dressing of well-rotted manure or compost every three years at the most, should do for most shrubs. It is only those such as roses, which are pruned hard each year, that may need to be fed annually. All shrubs, however, do appreciate the effects of regular mulching with bark or hay, or other suitable material.

Annual flowers

These should not need any additional feeding on a reasonable soil; too much encouragement tends to lead to lots of leafy growth and not much flower!

Fruit

Strawberries: these are not very demanding plants. A reasonable soil which has been lightly composted at planting time should suffice, with an additional mulch of leaf mould every spring.

Red and white currants, gooseberries, apples, plums, pears, cherries: a mulch of compost or manure every four to five years should be sufficient unless growth is poor. They will all benefit from a moisture-holding mulch such as leaf mould (or hay or straw) in the interim.

Blackcurrants, raspberries, hybrid berries: pruning removes a considerable proportion of these plants each year, so they may need a richer soil than other fruits. Mulch with compost or manure every three years or so, and with other materials in the intervening years.

Trees and hedges

These should not need manure or compost. They do however benefit from a thick mulch in the first season to help establishment by keeping the soil moist and discouraging weeds.

Lawns

If feeding is required, a dressing of fine compost can be given in the spring or summer. Leaf mould makes an excellent soil conditioner, spread over the lawn and chopped finely with the mower. Also finely shredded bark may be used.

Tubs, window boxes, pots and other containers

Established boxes and containers can be given a boost by topping them up with approximately 1 cm of well-rotted compost. The richness and texture of worm compost makes it particularly good in this instance.

Potting composts

Compost, worm compost and leaf mould can all be used as ingredients of home-made potting composts. The quality of the compost will have some bearing on the final performance of the final product, but the following recipes make a good starting point:

2 parts compost
1 part good loam
1 part peat/fine bark mix or well-rotted leaf mould

or

3 parts worm compost
1 part sedgepeat
1 part perlite

or

1 part worm compost
1 part peat/leaf mould
1 part perlite
1 part good garden loam

Straw, hay and woodland materials

Hay, straw, shredded prunings and bark can play a useful part in a soil building campaign, used in a fresh or semi-composted state. They make excellent soil protecting, weed controlling mulches which will last a lot longer than compost. They could, of course, be mixed with other ingredients and recycled through a compost heap (though this would take some time in the case of wood chips and bark) but their very toughness makes them of value as they stand, as long as they are used as surface mulches only. If they are dug into the soil there is a risk of nitrogen robbery.

It is necessary to treat some of these materials before they are used. Hay and straw should be left to weather for six months or so, (unless they are from organic sources), to give weedkiller residues time to decompose. Purchased 'woodland mulches' (mainly shredded twigs and branches) and bark products should have been composted before they are sold. This process will have killed any diseases, and also driven off compounds such as phenols which can inhibit plant growth. If you have a shredder and can produce your own mulching material, heap it up to allow it to heat up before use, or put it through the compost heap.

Hay
This will supply plant foods as it decays and will improve soil structure. Suitable for use on annual and perennial crops.

Straw
This lasts longer than hay, but supplies fewer plant foods. Suitable for use on annual and perennial crops. Remove remaining straw before cultivating the soil.

Woodland mulch/shredded bark
These are so tough and slow to decay, that they should only be used on perennial

Wood chips make attractive mulches and can give excellent long term weed control.

plantings, or where the soil will not be disturbed. There is no danger of nitrogen robbery if used in this way. If the soil is poor, feed it before adding the mulch.

Home shredded prunings
As these are relatively soft materials they decompose quicker than bark etc., but are probably still best used on perennials. They can benefit both soil structure and fertility, though how much will depend on what has been shredded. Conifer and evergreen prunings can be used if they are well rotted, preferably mixed with other materials. They tend to produce a rather acid material.

If these mulches are primarily for weed control, layers of bark or wood chips should be about 10 cm deep. More open materials, such as straw or hay, need thicker layers, unless the ground is first covered with newspaper, or something similar, to exclude the light. Keep them topped up as they decompose.

Green manures

Green manures are unlike the other materials covered in this book in that they are not waste products of home, farm or garden. They are in fact types of plants, such as clovers, mustard, rye and trefoil, (*see pages 41–43*), and are included here because they are grown specifically to benefit soil structure and fertility. Their regular use can have a remarkable effect on the soil and the plants that grow in it.

Green manures have been a traditional part of agriculture for centuries and they still play an important role in organic farming. They have not been widely used in private and market gardens, probably because they are looked upon as a waste of valuable space. But, as a good soil is the basis of effective organic growing, a crop grown to benefit that soil is certainly *not* a waste of space. This is especially true of gardens where supplies of manure, compost and other organic materials may be hard to come by.

The process of green manuring is quite simple. Seeds are sown, the plants allowed to grow for a length of time, and then they are dug back into the soil. There they decompose, releasing the foods they contain to the plants that follow on. This may sound like a pointless exercise, but the benefits will become clear as you read on!

When and where to grow green manures

Green manures can be sown at most times of the year. Choose one that is appropriate to the season and to the time that is available before the land is needed again. The various types of green manures available and their particular attributes are described on pages 41–45.

Quick summer green manures

During the growing season, a quick green manure such as mustard, fenugreek or buckwheat can be fitted in at various times: before sowing a main crop of carrots for example, or before planting out courgettes or winter brassicas. A site that is to be planted up with

---

WHY GROW GREEN MANURES?

To protect the soil

● The average garden or allotment often has some bare patches, especially over the winter months. A bare soil may deteriorate: a green manure cover crop will protect it.

● Whenever the soil is warm enough, microbes will be at work breaking down organic material and releasing plant foods. This can continue late into autumn when a green manure can be grown to take up these plant foods (which would otherwise be washed out by rain) and store them for use by subsequent crops.

● Heavy rains can have a harmful effect on the structure of the soil surface and, in extreme cases, cause erosion. A covering of green manure will protect it.

● A bushy green manure is ideal for suppressing weeds.

To improve the soil

● Green manures use air and sunlight to grow quantities of organic material which will, in turn, improve soil structure.

● Some green manures, called nitrogen fixers, can take up nitrogen from the air. This is stored in nodules in their roots and is available to subsequent plants when the green manure decomposes.

● Green manures have extensive root systems which help soil structure. Some are fine and fibrous; these help to break up clays and bind sands. Others go very deep and help to improve drainage, as well as bringing up minerals from depths that many other plants do not reach.

fruit or shrubs in the autumn or winter months can benefit from a month or two of green manuring.

Green manures over winter

Green manures are particularly beneficial when sown in late summer/early autumn. This is when most people will dig their land and then leave it bare until the following spring. But at this time of year the soil is still warm and the soil life is still actively releasing plant foods. These will be washed out by the winter rains unless a green manure is grown to take them up. Winter hardy types such as clovers, tares, and grazing rye are usually chosen for late summer and autumn sowing. They grow over the winter and are dug in the following year. Heavy soils can make conditions impossible for digging in, in which case grow one of the less hardy green manures, such as fenugreek or buckwheat, which will be killed off by the winter frosts.

Longer term green manures

Soil will benefit greatly from 'resting' under a green manure for a summer, or even a whole year. Incorporating a green manure plot into the rotation in a vegetable garden is worthwhile, as is resting a bed in the ornamental garden. Green manures can look very attractive too!

Growing compost material

A bed put down to a perennial green manure, such as alfalfa, for a few years can yield a useful source of compost and mulching material, at the same time benefitting the soil where it is growing. Alfalfa can be cut several times in one year, and will last several years if required. Red clover can also be used in this way, though it is not as productive.

Reclaiming a garden

Green manures are also useful when reclaiming an old garden, or creating a new one. If land has been broken up but not planted, they can be growing and improving the soil *and* keeping weeds in check. A quick green manure such as mustard, which needs a good soil to do well, can be a good indicator of the fertility of the soil.

Growing green manures

Soil

Green manures will grow best on a fertile soil – one manured or composted for a previous crop is ideal. If the soil is poor, choose an appropriate variety.

Sowing

Green manure seed can be sown in rows, or broadcast over the ground and raked in. Broadcast sowing is easier for very small seeds such as clovers, trefoil and alfalfa. These seeds can be mixed with sand or bone meal to help spread them thinly. Row sowing is the better method for the larger seeded beans, lupins etc. Others can be sown either way.

Broadcast sowing
- gives an even cover.
- it is quicker than sowing in rows, especially over large areas.

Row sowing
- takes longer
- allows deeper sowing, which is essential for larger seeds (e.g. lupin or tares) that require more moisture to germinate.
- helps to hide seeds from birds (important in the case of grazing rye).
- makes future hoeing simpler.
- tends to use less seed.

Undersowing

Farmers often sow a green manure at the same time as a cereal, so when the cereal is harvested in the autumn, the green manure is already established and ready to give a good winter cover. This technique, known as undersowing, can also be used in the garden providing the green manure does not compete with the crop. A low growing green manure such as trefoil, sown broadcast under a sweet corn crop, when the corn is a few inches high, can work well. Undersowing Brussels sprouts can also succeed. It is a technique well worth experimenting with in the garden.

How long should you grow green manures for?

A green manure should be sown with the aim of digging it in a few weeks before the land is required for other uses. As growing conditions are unpredictable it is not always possible to achieve this, and the stage of growth of the green manure may be a more compelling factor in deciding when to dig it in.

For maximum benefit, a green manure should be left to grow for as long as possible, turning it in just before it starts to get slightly woody and tough. With annuals, this is usually when the flowers begin to open. If a perennial green manure begins to flower, but the land is not needed for a while, it should be cut down to encourage new fresh growth.

Once green manure plants have become tough and woody they will be harder to dig in; they will take longer to decompose in the soil and there is always the danger of nitrogen robbery. The answer is to cut the foliage down, leaving it as a mulch, or recycle it through the compost heap.

Of course green manures can also be dug in before they have reached the 'ideal' stage.

Preparing the ground for future planting

Digging in
The simplest way to deal with a green manure is to turn it back into the soil, using a sharp spade. It should not be buried too deeply – no more than 15 cm on a heavy soil, or 20 cm on a light soil. Any deeper and the lack of air may inhibit the soil organisms that decompose the green manure; it may also be out of reach of the plants that are to follow on. Young, lush, green manures should be easy to deal with and usually need only be turned in once. Older, tougher plants will need more effort to incorporate them sufficiently, especially if the following crop needs a fine seed bed.

No-dig methods
It is quite possible to deal with a green manure without digging at all!

> **How to make digging in easier**
> ● Mow the green manures before digging.
> ● Scythe, or cut down, the green manure plants, leaving the foliage on the soil surface to wilt for a day or two before digging.
> ● Chop up the plants (tops and roots) with a sharp spade while digging in.
> ● Turn the green manure roughly; leave it for a few days before digging the land over again.
> ● Cover the green manure with a light-excluding mulch for a few weeks before digging.

You can hoe off annual green manures, leaving the plants *in situ* as a mulch to be taken into the soil by the worms.

You can chop or mow down the green manure, then plant into the remaining 'stubble'. Manures that are likely to regrow, (perennial green manures and grazing rye for example), can be killed out by the use of a light-excluding mulch, such as black polythene or newspaper. Transplants can be planted through this if desired.

You can sow a frost-tender green manure in late summer, so that it will be killed off by the winter cold.

Planting after a green manure
Once a green manure has been dug in, some time must elapse before the ground can be used again, because decomposition must get well underway, and the ground be allowed to settle. Take this time lag into account when deciding where and when to grow green manures.

How long a time-lag depends on several factors: the maturity of the plants, how much they are chopped up, and the temperature of the soil. The turn-around from a tender mustard crop in midsummer can be as little as a week; a period of three or four weeks may be needed for more mature, unchopped plants in a cold, heavy soil.

The type of plant that is to follow also has a bearing on when to plant. If you require a fine tilth for seed sowing it will take longer to achieve than a rougher bed for transplanting.

If a green manure has been dug in and the ground is not going to grow anything for a couple of months or more, another green manure should be grown – or all that goodness contained in the first one will be lost!

Plants for green manuring

See notes on page 44.

Alfalfa *(Medicago sativa)*

A very deep rooting plant. Foliage contains an excellent range of plant foods. If growing long term, cut down two or three times a year to encourage growth.

Related to trefoil and other legumes.

Sow broadcast at the rate of 2–3 g per sq metre.

Buckwheat *(Fagopyrum esculentum)*

An attractive plant with red stems and unusual shaped leaves. Deep rooter. Tiny pink flowers which hoverflies love. Very frost sensitive.

Related to Polygonum species.

Sow broadcast at the rate of 10 g per sq metre.

Beans, winter field *(Vicia faba)*

An agricultural variety of the broad bean, usually grown for animal feed. Does not control weeds unless sown closely. Can be cut down and left to re-grow once – a useful trick if plants have toughened.

Related to winter tares, broad beans and other legumes.

Sow beans 10 cm apart in rows 15–20 cm apart.

Clover, red and alsike *(Trifolium spp)*

Similar plants, one with white flowers and the other red. Much loved by bees. Red clover is more bushy and deeper rooting. Prone to drought.

Related to Trifolium clovers and other legumes.

Sow both broadcast 2–3 g per sq metre.

Clover, crimson *(Trifolium incarnatum)*

A vigorous quick growing clover, with wonderful red flowers, which bees love.

Related to Trifolium clovers and other legumes.

Sow broadcast 2–3 g per sq metre.

Bitter Lupin *(Lupinus angustifolius)*

Smaller than the traditional garden lupin. A very deep rooter with blue flowers. Seeds must be well covered.

Related to other legumes.

Sow 3–4 cm deep and 5–10 cm apart in rows 10–20 cm apart.

Mustard *(Sinapis alba)*

One of the quickest growing green manures. Yellow flowers. Once flowers form it gets tough quickly. Susceptible to clubroot.

Related to the cabbage family, wallflowers and other crucifers.

Sow broadcast at the rate of 3–5 g per sq metre.

Fenugreek *(Trigonella foenum graecum)*

An attractive quick growing bushy plant with insignificant white flowers, and a mass of foliage.

Related to other legumes.

Sow broadcast 5 g per sq metre.

Phacelia (Phacelia tanacetifolia)

A lovely bush plant with masses of fern-like foliage and bright blue flowers which bees love. Keeps weeds down well. Seeds can be expensive but it is easy to save your own.

Sow broadcast at the rate of 2–3 g per sq metre.

Trefoil (Medicago lupilina)

One of the lower growing legumes. Easy to grow; has small yellow flowers in the first or second season. Tolerates some shade and drought, so is suitaable for undersowing.

Related to alfalfa and other legumes.

Sow broadcast at the rate of 1½–3 g per sq metre.

Rye, grazing (Secale cereale)

A cereal rye, not rye grass. Its extensive root system makes it one of the best for soil structure improvement. Grows fast in early spring and is one of the most effective green manures.

Sow broadcast at the rate of 30 g per sq metre.

Tares, winter (Vicia sativa)

A rapid growing annual vetch. Good bushy plants, which control weeds well once established. Likes heavy, alkaline soils and cannot stand drought. Can be mixed with grazing rye. Seed must be well covered to germinate.

Related to broad beans, field beans and other legumes.

Sow broadcast at the rate of 20 g per sq metre, or in rows 4–5 cm deep, 15 cm apart.

Green manures – at a glance

Plant	Annual (A) Perennial (P) Biennial (B)	Hardy (H) Semi Hardy (SH) Tender (T)	Approx. maximum height	Duration
Alfalfa *Medicago sativa*	P	H	150 cm	Long
Beans, winter field *Vicia faba*	A	H	90 cm	Overwinter
Buckwheat *Fagopyrum esculentum*	A	T	80 cm	Short/Medium
Clover, Alsike *Trifolium hybridum*	P	H	30 cm	Medium/Long
Clover, crimson *Trifolium incarnatum*	A	SH	60 cm	Medium
Clover, Essex red *Trifolium pratense*	P	H	40 cm	Medium/Long
Fenugreek *Trigonella foenum graecum*	A	SH	60 cm	Short/Medium
Lupin, bitter *Lupinus angustifolius*	A	SH	50 cm	Medium
Mustard *Sinapis alba*	A	T–SH	90 cm	Short
Phacelia *Phacelia tanacetifolia*	A	SH–H	90 cm	Short/Medium
Rye, grazing *Secale cereale*	A	H	60 cm	Overwinter
Tares, winter *Vicia sativa*	A	H	75 cm	Medium/Overwinter
Trefoil *Medicago lupulina*	A/B	H	60 cm	Medium/Long

Notes for green manure pictures

Related to: some green manures are related to other types of green manure and to commonly grown vegetables. It is important to know this when planning a crop rotation system.

Sowing rates: there is room for some variation. The more fertile the soil and the longer the growth period of the green manure, the lower the rate required. Increase the rate for a quick, thick cover.

Notes for green manure chart

Duration

Short: use where a green manure cover is needed for a month or two in the spring and summer. They are quick to start and will grow rapidly. Those marked 'short' will go tough quickly once they start to flower. Those marked 'short/medium' are slower to mature.

Medium: use where a green manure cover is needed for two to three months during the main growing season.

Overwinter: varieties suitable for late summer/early autumn sowing, to be dug in the following spring. Varieties marked 'long' will of course also survive the winter.

Long: grow for a year or more. Can usually be cut several times a year.

H/SH/T

H: should survive most winters.
SH: will stand a mild winter.
T: will be killed by the first hard frost.

Soil type	Nitrogen fixing	When to sow	Digging in
Dislikes acid or waterlogged soils; will survive quite dry conditions once established	No. Unless appropriate bacteria added	Apr to July	Any time when fresh and green. Hard work
Prefers heavy land, will not tolerate drought	Yes	Sept to Nov	Any time up to flowering. Average
Will tolerate poor soils	No	Mid Mar to Aug	Any time up to flowering. Easy
Will stand wetter, more acid soils than most clovers	Yes	Apr to Aug	Average
Prefers a sandy loam. Dislikes heavy soil	Yes	Mar to Aug	Before flowering. Average
Avoid poor soils. Prefers a good loam	Yes	Apr to Aug	Any time when fresh and green. Average
Best on well drained but slightly heavy soils	Not normally	Mar to Aug	Before pods form. Easy
One of the best for light, slightly acid soils	Yes	Mar to June	Before flowers open Average
Reasonably moist and fertile soil	No	Mar to mid Sept	Any time up to flowering. Easy
Average	No	Mar to mid Sept	Before flowers open. Easy
Most	No	Aug to Nov	When flower heads begin to form in base of plant. Hard work
Slightly heavy soils preferred. Will not thrive on dry or acid soils	Yes	Mar to May July to Sept	Up to flowering. Average
Will stand light dry soils, preferably neutral to alkaline	Yes	Mar to Aug	Any time when fresh and green. Average

Conclusion

Compost, manures and other organic materials, along with green manures, can have a considerable influence on the health and productivity of a garden. They all provide plant foods to a greater or lesser extent, but more importantly they will all have a positive effect on the structure of the soil.

But this isn't the whole organic story. Not everyone will be able to make enough compost and collect enough manure for the garden, especially in the early stages of becoming organic. In this situation there is a range of organic fertilisers, such as blood, fish and bone meal, and dried seaweed, which can be used to supply fertility.

It is also very important to get to know your soil, and to learn how to manage it in the best possible way, rather than making blind assumptions which could so easily be wrong. Factors such as soil type, drainage and management regime can all influence the productivity of a garden. A lot of useful information can be garnered by feeling and looking at the soil, but some important details such as pH and mineral status can only be discovered by having the soil analysed in a laboratory.

These other aspects of managing a soil organically are beyond the scope of this particular volume, but are dealt with in another book in the same series on soil care. By reading these books and following the guidelines contained in them, you will, in time, have a beautiful garden that is teeming with wildlife and full of healthy fruit, vegetables and flowers.

Glossary

Brassicas: cabbages, Brussels sprouts, cauliflowers, kale, borecole, turnips, swedes, cress, salad, rape and mustards. All are closely related and are members of the 'Brassica' family of plants.

Broadcast sowing: scattering seeds in an even pattern over the soil surface, rather than sowing in rows.

Carbon: a major element in the make up of plants; tough, fibrous parts are rich in carbon.

Drill: narrow, shallow depression made in the soil by edge of rake or other tool, for sowing seed into.

Heavy metals: elements found in the soil and in some manures and sewage. Those that are of interest to gardeners include copper, zinc, iron and cadmium. High levels may be toxic to plants and to people.

Legumes: peas, beans, clovers and other related crops.

Lime: a powder formed by crushing or processing limestone rock. Lime makes soil and compost more alkaline (see above).

Liquid manure: a liquid plant food made by steeping certain plant leaves, manure or compost in water.

Major elements: a plant's food supply must contain a wide range of different elements. The ones that are needed in the greatest quantity, the major elements, are nitrogen, phosphorus and potassium (often known as potash).

Mulch: any material spread over the soil.

Nitrogen: one of the most important plant foods; nitrogen is used in particular to grow leaves and shoots.

Nitrogen fixer: the air is full of nitrogen and some bacteria, known as nitrogen fixers, are able to take it up. Plants such as peas and beans have these bacteria living in their roots, and can use the nitrogen that the bacteria extract from the air.

Organic: a method of growing plants which avoids the use of chemical pesticides and artificial fertilisers. Instead, it relies on crop rotation, recycling crop residues through a compost heap, slow acting ground rock minerals, animal manures and waste products and green manures to keep the soil fertile. Pests, weeds and diseases are controlled by the encouragement of natural control organisms means. Organic methods aim to minimise disruption of the natural environment.

Index Chapter headings are in bold type.